Walkthrough

Let's look at the front cover. Read the title. What do you think this story might be about? Where do you think the story takes place?

Walkthrough

Let's turn to the back cover and read the blurb. Who do you think says 'Booooo!'?

Walkthrough

Read the title with me again. What do you think this little boy is saying to the girl? Remember the title of our book.

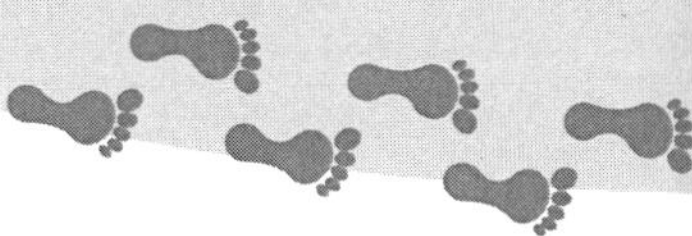

Walkthrough

Introduce the main characters' names.

Why does Josh want to talk to Beth?

Observe and Prompt

Word Recognition

Ⓟ Encourage the children to use their decoding skills to read 'Quick', 'bent', 'head' and 'next'. Can they spot the three words with the same short 'e' phoneme? How is this phoneme spelt in each word?

● The words 'message' and 'I've' may not be decodable for children at this stage. If they struggle with these words, model reading them for the children.

Walkthrough

Beth bent down so her head was next to Josh's. What do you think Josh said to her?

I bent my head next to his . . .

3

Observe and Prompt

Language Comprehension

- Encourage the children to predict what might happen next.

Walkthrough

What does Josh say? Point to the speech bubble.

How do you think Beth is feeling now?

4

 **Observe and Prompt**

Word Recognition

● Check the children can independently read the sight word
'said'.

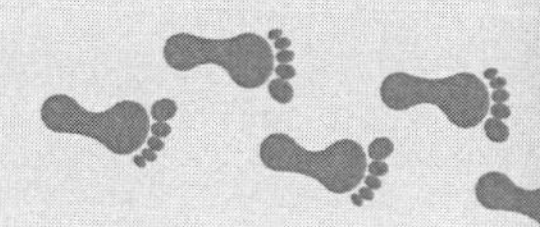

5

Observe and Prompt

Language Comprehension

● Encourage the children to use appropriate expression when reading 'Booooo!'

Walkthrough

Jill is calling Beth over now. What do you think she wants to say to her?

Observe and Prompt

Word Recognition

P Check that the children can sound out and blend the phonemes all through the words 'Jill', 'Look', 'tell', 'bent' 'head', 'next'. If they struggle with 'something', model how to split it into syllables and read each syllable in turn.

P How many words on these two pages have the short 'e' phoneme as in 'next'? (five – 'said', 'tell', 'bent', 'head', 'next')

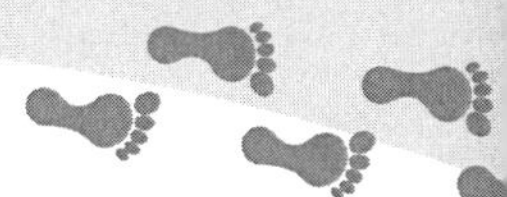

I bent my head next to hers . . .

7

 **Observe and Prompt**

Language Comprehension

- How does Beth feel now? How would the children feel if they were her?

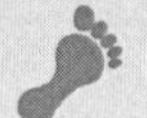

Walkthrough

What does Jill say? Why do you think Josh and Chen are laughing?
How do you think Beth feels now?

 **Observe and Prompt**

Word Recognition

(P) Can the children segment and write another word with the 'oo' sound that rhymes with 'Boo'?

Language Comprehension

● Check that the children understand that, so far, the joke is on Beth.

8

 **Walkthrough**

Where is Beth now? Who wants to whisper to her? What do you think might happen next?

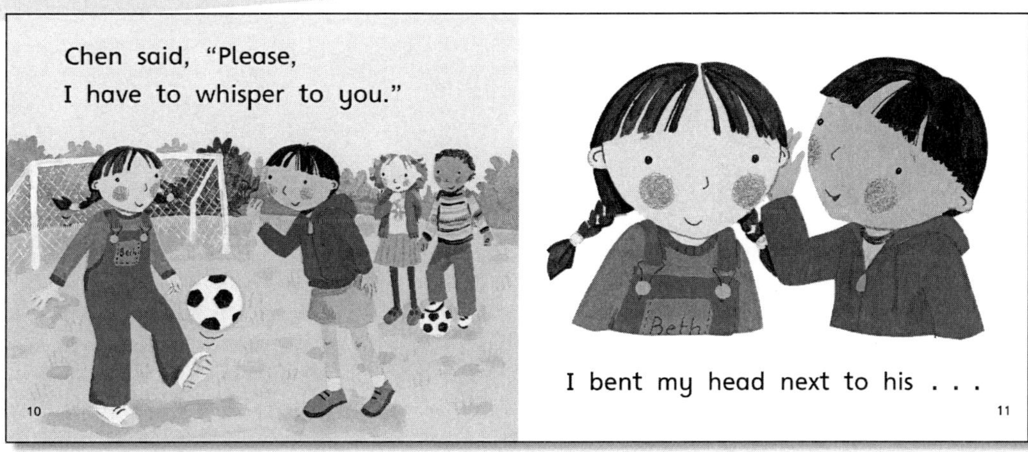

Observe and Prompt

Word Recognition

(P) Encourage the children to read the words by sounding out and blending the phonemes in order.

- If the children struggle with 'whisper', model how to read this word for them.

Language Comprehension

- Can the children read what Chen says in a whisper, with appropriate intonation?

 **Walkthrough**

What do you think might happen next?

 **Observe and Prompt**

Word Recognition

(P) Can the children show you the word that has the short 'e' phoneme on these pages ('said')?

Language Comprehension

- Ask the children how they would feel if they were Beth. What would they do?

Walkthrough

What do you think the friends are trying to tell Beth now?
Do you think she's going to be tricked again? What do you think
she's going to do?

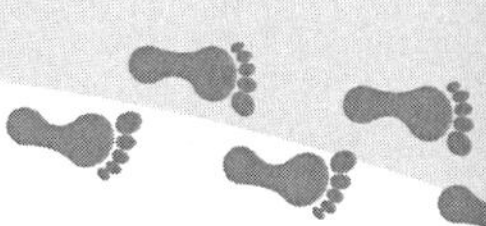

Observe and Prompt

Word Recognition

(P) Check that children use
their decoding skills to
read the words 'Then',
'them', 'rush', 'thing', 'tell',
'bent', 'head', 'next'.

● The other words are sight
words – can the children
read them independently?
If necessary, help them to
read 'theirs'.

Language Comprehension

● Check that children
recognise the use of the
exclamation mark and use
appropriate intonation.

Walkthrough

What is Beth saying? How is she feeling now? How are her friends feeling?

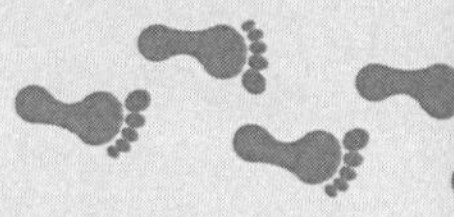

and I said, "BOOOOOOOO!"

16

 **Observe and Prompt**

Language Comprehension

- Check that the children understand that Beth has now returned the joke.